COMPUTERS IN SOCIETY

Dr. Iwasan Kejawa

World of Science and Technology

****

COMPUTERS   IN   SOCIETY

World of Science and Technology

Dr. Iwasan D. Kejawa

Contents

Foreword

Acknowledgement

Introduction

- Types of Computers

Modern Usage of Computers

- Using Computers in Business

- Science Applications of Computers

- Technology Applications of Computers

- Using Computers in Education

Computer Development Strategy

- Education Strategy
- Technology Strategy

Functions of Computers

- Intellectual Function of Computers
- Capability Function of Computers

Longevity of Computers

- Memory and Physical Attributes

Summary

- Epilogue

FOREWARD

This book is for everyone who is interested in the studies of computers and those who will like to explore the technology world. The book can serve as a repertoire and ingredient for basic computer literacy. The basic social aspects of using computer were refined in this book paraphernalia. The book may be use as introduction to social aspects of computers by an audience of little or average knowledge of computers. The book can be used in conjunction with other books of computer science and engineering subjects or courses in secondary schools and freshman year in universities and colleges.

%%
%%
%%
%%
%%
%%
%%
%%

ACKNOWLEDGEMENT

My Sincere thanks to those that contributed to the publication of this work.

INTRODUCTION

This book explore what computers are, their usages and their functionalities. Computers can be used to learn or comprehend the understanding of all subjects, be it physics, aerobics, swimming, biology, mathematics, agriculture, chemistry, business administration or commerce, just to name a few. In education, computers are used to project information to individuals in the classrooms or anywhere education is taking place, in churches, homes, schools, conference halls and so on. It is also used to convey the logic of a subject or behind a topic. Computers play an important role in educating our mind. With the usage of computers, we are able to learn, we are able to devise new ways of doing things.

The use of computers in education allows us to convey instructions or ideas by all means. Globalizations of the entities comprising the learning processes are the computer configurations in actual facts.

TYPES

Types of Computers

There are various types of computers in the today's global market. The first calculating device was invented by Charles Babbage, a Mathematician; and this device is known as Abacus which led to the invention of computers. If one looks immensely on what we mean by computers or what computers are, one may say that all entities of the world are computers. The inventions of computers are based on inferences and inductive thinking. Without human knowledge computers cannot function. We as human beings depend on computers to perform sophisticated tasks that we cannot perform; and somehow one has to instruct or program the computer to carry out or perform our desire functions.

We have computers of the centuries ago and computers of today, and those of the future in progress. Actually there are two types of computers come to functionality. We have analogue and digital computers. Digital computers may be termed as electronic devices; they are computers without fluidity. They function with the flow of atmosphere whereas analogue types of computers depend on physical attributes of the atmosphere.

Most of the analogue computers are of ages; they are built more than two to four centuries ago whereas digital computers are of the modern version. This is not to say that digital computers had not been in existence years ago. There are generations of computers which are up six or more generations. Computers are the extensions of the mind physically and mentally. Analogue computers could be considered to be mental or analogy entities and digital computer to be physical or visual or literary entities. Basically, analogue computers are the types of computers which solve problems intrinsically by leaving the solutions afloat. With analogue computers one has to use deductive rather than inductive thinking to arrive at a final or desire solution while digital computers give one the actual solution or direct answer. We also have computers that are combinations of analogues and digitals in the modern society. These types of computers are embedded computers such as refrigerators, microwave oven, cars, bathroom scales, just to name a few.

All technological equipment is to be considered computers of some sort. We now have digital computer markers, pens, phones, drinking glasses, televisions, printers, and handheld devices. Some analogue computers are electric water dams, rotary phones, analogue watches, typewriters and bicycles. Computers have come a long way and the evolution of the technology has surpassed human endearments. Technology has the entities of foreseen products around the world. As long as we built bridges between intellectual education experts in the field of technology, there will be a robust growth in the development and manufacturing of computers. The flood of the global market with different types of computers will continue thus driving prices down;

this will also create an enormous growth in the usage of computers. More people will have access to owning a computer as progress through the ages. And there will be an increase innovative processes. Discovery of new ideas may be put to use by people. People will be able to interact with one another due to the fluctuation of the excess use of computers.

Computers are essential commodities in the society because they tend to make one's life easy. Most functions that cannot be performed by humans are perform by computers. The basis for using computers is to extend the human mind beyond the normal process. Computers have come of ages; they have come in different sizes and they perform sophisticated tasks no matter what sizes they are physically. What really matters is the size of the computer memory to accommodate all the functions that need to be performed.

APPLICATIONS

MODERN USAGE OF COMPUTERS

Nowadays, the uses or applications of computer are becoming more rampant and ludicrous in terms of their simplicities and sophistications in all fields of Science, Engineering, Business and Arts. The coming age would definitely mandate the knowledge of the use of computers because of the innovation of technology, as the world changes. One must therefore be aware of the changes in technology in our world, so to speak. The negative perceptions of the usage of computers would eventually damage the invigorations and purpose of learning and innovation in our world.

Electronic applications of computers are the willingness to control the situations around the globe. In order to sharply increase example-nary proprietaries using computers, we must know when, where and how to applied technology and formulas or algorithms. The innovative process of mathematical formulas in the applications of computers or technology would have an impact on the behavioral of the populace. One of the technicalities of the impact of innovation is to invigorate exposure to the usage of technologies, including computers. The applications of computers may have to involve acquiring necessary skills, experience and practice. The provisions of simple and not sophisticated computers will certainly improvise the business and scientific applications as well as technical applications. With computers we can easily solve problems precisely. Computers are often applied to the derivations of solutions which are not made aware of to everyone.

The development and application of computers are through innovation and satisfying the needs of humans. The scientific world is part of an elongated development and applications of computers. And it can be substantiated with the use and evolution of computers and technologies. Applications of computers are the entities that comprise the need to achieve the ultimate goal of science in our world today. Computers are the conglomeration of scientific technologies.

The scientific world plays a role in the development of computers. It can be said that science is based on strategic planning. In the early evolutionary stage it has been noted through history that ideas and inventions can be obtained through exploration and scientific abomination. Technology is the foundation of the continuity, sustainability and transformations in the society. We can achieve our needs through critical innovation of technology regardless of our roles in society. We must have the knowledge base of using computers or technology, since we do not have control over what is to be learned. The circumstances surrounding the use technology and its development may be due to affordability and security - These may in turns affect their volatility and flexibility.

Computers play an important aspect of our lives because they may be used for just our daily chores. They are used by almost everyone. Computers are used by teachers, cooks, students, farmers, housewives, technicians, priests, aviators and medical doctors, just to mention a few. Almost all professions use some sorts or some kind of computer to perform function.

Using Computers for Business

Although many businesses use computers to solve business problems and to make decisions; we still need have to formulate how to interpret the business solutions from these computers. Some computers of today allow managers and employees to formulate mathematical algorithms that are used to resolve problems or make decisions. In the banking industries for example computers are used to calculate or process customers' transactions, and in the insurance companies, computers are used for projections and annuity calculations. Many large businesses depend on the use of computers to survive in the world of today. The benefits of using computers to solve problems outweigh their risks. To solve problem, we must first of formulate the problem by creating algorithms or formula and then use our intuitions to manipulate, solve or process the data or the information relating to the problem. Today instead of using our intuitions, most of the businesses use computers to solve problems in all their endeavors: Accounting, Production Management, Finance, Sales, Human Resources and Operations Management, and so forts are some of the areas computers are applied or used by businesses.

Science Applications of Computers

Computers are used by scientists for many scientific functions. They are used for predictions and solving problems of physical and unphysical entities or scenarios. They can be used for example to derive the amount of intake of oxygen in species in a period of time for example. Scientists applied computers in the same manner as a business man and technician or engineer. The creations of scientific computers have made life easier for mankind. The use of computers to solving scientist problems has made the world a better place to explore various ways of doing things and surviving on earth. For example, scientists have made use of computer to prolong human lives both physiologically and mentally. Scientific applications of computers actually lead to progression of human existence, and the physical being itself. For example, computers can be used to measure the amount of granules a plant would need to grow normally and how many times the plant supposed to be fed. Computers serve various functions in the scientific world. Scientists use computers just as businesspersons or entrepreneurs use computers to carry out or perform their daily functions. Scientific applications of computers enable engineers to design physical entities, predict and implement most functions.

Technology Applications of Computers

The use of computers is very common in engineering. For example in the designs of bridges, automobiles, robots, houses and so on, just to mention a few. An example of the usage of computers by engineer in building a bridge is to find the capacity and the length of the proposed bridge by measurement. In manufacturing automobile for example: the engineers may use computers to predict how fast they would like an automobile to travel and the amount of gas it will consume or use before even manufacturing the automobile. Also robots which can be classify as some kind of computers are now being used to assemble parts in automobile industry and some other kind of manufacturing industries. The technology application of computers is sophisticated because it requires using agents of what or that constitute computer itself. The implementation of all aspect of computers dwells on substance or problem.

Using Computers in Education

Educational applications of computer rest solely on what is to be achieved. Computers are used to satisfy the intricacies of human mind. Computers are used to comprehend what is not known to us. They are used to embellish the ultimate performance of existentiality. Computers can be used to initiate, update and retain knowledge.

Computers can be used to learn or comprehend the understanding of all subjects, be it physics, aerobics, swimming, biology, mathematics, agriculture, chemistry, business administration or commerce, just to name a few. In education, computers are used to project information to individuals in the classrooms or anywhere education is taking place, in churches, homes, schools, conference halls and so on. It is also used to convey the logic of a subject or behind a topic. Computers play an important role in educating our mind. With the usage of computers we are able to learn, we are able to devise new ways of doing things. The use of computers in education allows us to convey instructions or ideas by all means. Globalizations of the entities comprising the learning processes are protrude by using computers.

STRATEGIES

STRATEGIC DEVELOPMENTS OF COMPUTERS

The strategy of the development of computers is to ease the ways we doing things in life. It is to eliminate the obstacles of living on the planet and to prevent or secure substantial endurance of humans. It is to alleviate all the problems encounter in everyday life.

Education Strategy

The issues of reaching a diverse populace with online distance education are very important issues in the educational institution environments today. With the increased in the number of institutions providing online distance education to the society, it is becoming an alarming issue as to whether educational institutions are reaching or serving a diverse population.

The criteria of providing online distance computer education technology are to better serve the entire population and providing leadership in education. But are educational institution actually reaching the entire population or only a segment of the population is being reached?

Societal factors such as economic maladies and unawareness of technological innovations may prevent educational institution from attaining the goal of serving the entire population with the online distances education, and thus establishing leadership in education. The issue focus is that with the practices and introduction of computer online education, certain segment of the population may not being catered for. This part of the population is the group of minorities who could not afford the cost of computer technologies attached to online education. Also another segment of the population that may not be reached by online education is the group who is not aware of the innovated online distance computer technological education.

Even though there have being an increased in the use of technology in recent years, only certain segment of the population still could afford to own computers. According to the article in Computerworld magazine, titled "A surge in the use computers", more than two billion computers were sold in the United States in the past years, and the majority of the buyers were the middle class. It was also mentioned that most people use their computers for business and personal chores or pleasures

With the improved computer technological innovations, there is introduction of online distance education into education curriculum. But with the costs associated with the purchase, services and internet set up, many individuals in the society could not still afford the online computer distance education. Distance online education through the internet is growing and expanding globally. The distance education strategy and training are becoming integrated as a whole unit rather than separate entities. More interdisciplinary abilities are now required and the new generations of students and educators are bringing diverse perspectives about life, work and family.

The driving forces for not reaching a diverse population with distance education may be attributed to economic reason and the high increase in tuition fees, and the still expensive computers. The majority of individual is poor and could not afford to own computers after meeting all other expenses. Tuitions and the costs of internet services and owning computers posed a great deal of problem to students who will like to participate in distance learning education.

If educational institutions can synthesize an appropriate strategic planning method for technology and distance learning computer education, there may well be explosive growth and evolution of innovations. There is presently competition among educational establishment on the provisions of online distance learning education. Educational institutions will face much tighter competition with the online distance learning based on new available technologies. We should be aware that those who adopt state-of-the-art methods will prosper and those who ignore them will eventually fail. If the universities can lower tuition and try to offer free computers and internet services to distance education students, then it will be able to succeed in reaching a diverse population of students across the globe with distance education technologies.

The issues of reaching a diverse population in the society with distance learning education and establishing leadership in education are vital and critical because tuition costs are increasing and technology continues to grow and impact the society. In order to avoid problems, good strategies and techniques are needed for planning, implementation and maintenance of technology. Without the appropriate planning and methods, institutions' online distance learning education programs may suffer. If many institutions are to cut tuition costs and provides each student with a personal computer and a free internet service, then the institutions will be able to satisfy their visions and missions.

Technology Strategy

The technological planning is based on what constitute technology in the modern society. There is a correlation between what is technology of the past, the present and the future. In today information age educational technology products are based on knowledge, values and pragmatic approach.

Technology management products are of great importance as well developing computers in the society. The past and present terms are reciprocity of the global markets. The retention of computers serves the purpose of conservatism and pragmatic values and approach. Change in the products and information are preserved in the society. This change is pragmatic to the management of the institutions or societies. The computer information age is a co-existence of values and desire. The philosophical entity of technology composed of resources and performance. The composition of information is the entity of educational products in the global market. The consistency of technological products is based on the magnitudes of the information obtained from the past and present.

Models and consistencies of technologies are aligned with extensive extenuation of objectivity in education. With the extenuation of objectives, there are subjectivities to innovations of computers. The past may be subjective to the development of the modern computers. Educational products and information are inter-changeable commodities in technological society. The aspect of globalization of computer technology is empowered through development of many external entities.

The configuration of external foreign technological entities, such as tools of the past era results in commonwealth of education technology. Technological posterity serves as the philosophical view of the modern. There is prosperity from modern ways of computing because of the convenience the technological innovations have portrayed. Information are internally and externally exposed and stored technologically. The value of information is the logical dwelling of philosophical abstracts of technology.

The transcendence of technology depends on innovations of both the present and past in order to attain simplicity of adaptability and more sophisticated technological amenities. This presents the future with lasting and endurance of educational technology tools in the society. Computer technology is adeptly the invigoration of educational expertise in our society. The combinations of know how, when and why would be attributed to the development and enhancement of computer tools and their awareness. We must adhere to the improvements of the previous and the modern as well as gear or prepare towards new developments of technology in the society. The strategic implementations of science and technology intentions would provide common grounds in the development of computers.

FUNCTIONS

FUNCTIONS OF COMPUTERS

Computers are believed to possess intelligence that surpasses that of humans. They are met to perform all the functions that are beyond human control. The exploration of science to achieve the ultimate goal of humans is an important aspect of computers. The belief instilled in the mind of society that computers cannot ultimately perform all human functions is actually misleading. The world of science provides a security of physical, psychological and social well beings of the populace. This plays a role in the development of fourth, fifth and sixth generation of computers. Computers are used for assimilation of knowledge of humans. And the functions carried out by super computers or the more intelligent computers are superb compare to that of humans if their designs and constructions or architectures are proper. It can be said that education is based on strategic planning in development of computers. In the early exploration of science, it has been noted through history that ideas and inventions can be obtained through rigorous training of the mind. The usage of computers is the continuity of sustainability and transformation of their developments. The education of humans can be the sole of beneficiary of the success of scientific exploration of the needs to justify the development of intelligent expert systems. It can be through critical innovation of the mind regardless of its role in the society. Everyone in the society is a learner since we have no control over what is to be learned. The society and individual determine what they want to learn and how we want to learn or use computers. The circumstances surrounding computer education and its mode of delivery may be due to affordability and security. These in turns affect the volatility and the flexibility of the usage of computers.

The needs to use computer and expert systems must be justify by the prosperity of societal factors. The incumbents of people involved in the development of expert systems or computers must have the resources of attaining their goals. The goals and needs of society must be deemed to include scenario of standard accomplishments with their expectations. The modalities of entities of understanding processes of humans must be convey to the world of science. The dexterity of the mind can be explained through all means of communications. Both internal and external modes of communication can be justified by individual in the society.

The processes of involvement in the functions of computers consist of spiritual processes and both physical and environmental processes. The uses of computers increase the progress of humans through the channel of dwelling of living. The society must be realized that education in the use of computers must be thoroughly explore and applied. The assumptions that we possess all the preliminary process of functioning without computers are absolutely not true. Computers are part of our daily lives. They are used nowadays to perform chores, be it cooking, reading, shopping at markets, worshiping at churches or harvesting at plantations. Computers or intelligent systems are no longer solely used by big corporations – they are everywhere. We as humans in the society tend to follow with a can-do all attitudes but knowledge always demand reflection. We absolutely can get to know ourselves if we take some quiet time to meditate as to how we use computers to solve problems in our daily life. One of the ways to learn to satisfy the society in use of computers is openness to suggestions and proper articulations of individual understanding of why we use science or technology or computers to solve problems. Mostly, scientific world is open to ideas and will try untested approaches, and accept risk in the exploration of ways of developing computers and the usage of computers. When we are at our personal best, our projects involve creative thinking and beyond-the-boundaries thinking because of the awareness of the functions of computer systems and its use. Even though development of computer has had impact in volume of their usage, it should be realized that nothing is done perfectly the very first time. We must also understand that as computers evolve through changes, we tend to search for opportunities to improve the sophistication of their usage. Opportunities that will meet the current changes and the foresee changes must be mandated in the scientific world. The future changes in the functions and usages of computers may depend on the learning materials of the present. The changes may involve physical, psychological and social changes which will impact their functions and usages by all sorts of people. Computer education rests on the hands of the beholder. Education in the usage of computers must be clarified by people in the society. We tend to learn as we progress through life based on the needs and consequences derived from the pasts. Mistakes are made and we all learn from our mistakes which is a form of education process. Results from the use of computer depend on perception of what is intended and the information fed into its memory.

It is to my beliefs that computer functions and their uses work wonders through developing of computer artifacts that justified the positive applications of computers.

Intellectual Function of Computers

Computers are able to function intellectually by applying the knowledge derived from humans. Human intellect is derived from spiritual creation whereas computer intellect may be said to be from that of human. It may then be inferred that both human intellectual function and that of computer are of spiritual means because human intellect is transfer to all artifacts.

The computers and other artifacts depend on the human ways of thinking. Without some human input computers will not function. For example, after assembling an automobile, dishwasher, printers, computer monitors, computer servers, radar, and other computer peripherals, without conveying to these artifacts or hardware to perform intellectually by humans it may not be possible for them to function. It is the living that tells the computer as to what to do and accomplish.

The core function of the computers is control by the information being fed to it by human. All non-living artifacts and some living artifacts relied sole on human way thinking to accomplish tasks. Mostly scientific world is open to ideas and will try untested approaches, and accept risk in the exploration of ways of developing computers and the usage of computers. When we are at our personal best, our projects will involve creative thinking and beyond-the-boundaries thinking because of awareness of the computer systems and its use. Even though the intellectual functions of computer has had impact in volume of their usage, it should be realized that the performance of computers depends on their configurations and programmed instructions. We must also understand that as computers evolve through changes of their pertinent memory and physical attributes or hardware. We tend to search for opportunities to improve the sophistication of computers usage and their developments. Usages and developments that will meet the current changes and the foresee changes which are in the scientific world. The future changes in the developments and usages of computers actually depend on the learning materials of the past and present.

Capability Function of Computers

Computers are capable of functions that are attributed to living things. They can perform absolutely any functions to ultimate level as required. They all served as entities of supremacy so to speak. Functions are carry out by computers according to instructions being fed into them. If bad information is fed then one will get back bad information in return; in order words "Garbage in Garbage Out". If we want to achieve ultimate result, then we must provide or feed computer with the input of information.

The function of computers may involve physical, psychological and social changes which will impact their usage by all sorts of people. The means of using computers rest on the hands of the beholder. Computers usage in educating the mind must be clarified by importance of the usage. We tend to learn and function as human beings by applying computers to various activities of our life. When using computers mistakes are made and we all learn from our mistakes which is a form of education process. Results from computer depend on its perception of what your intentions and information been fed into its memory.

It is to my beliefs that we can use computer to perform wonders through development of computer artifacts to justify the positive applications of computers.

LONGEVITY

DURABILITY OF COMPUTERS

It is believed that there will never be a ceased to the existence of computers. As long as the world is in place then computers will be in place. Actually the longevity of the attributes of computers are the homogeneity of their performance and physical attributes. As we continue to use computers and innovate technology, computers performance will continue to increase. To prolong the existence of computers, we as humans must devote our time in exploring all possible usages or applications of computers. The present entities are actually derived from the past and the present and past entities will continue to yield entities of the future. Computers are the fundamentals of human existentiality; without computers we as a society may not continue to survive.

The long haul of producing computers that are complex will lead to their conservation and improvement. Computers will always be in our mist no matter what the circumstances may be. The manufacturing of the future generations of computers rest on the hand of the beholders. Individual in the society will have to be responsible for the connotations attached to the development of computers as tools for human perseverance and human embodiment. Computers serve as the tools of the era, and the future of computers remains enlighten and positive.

Physical and Memory Attributes

Computers consist of peripherals as physical attributes. The physical attributes of computers are referred as hardware. Hardware may be termed as tangible physical components of the computer. The physical attributes depend on the main core of the computer to function as whole. Without the physical components or attributes, there will be no computers; and without the memory attributes, the physical component will not function properly. The components rely on the command issue by the memory of the computers. The difference between the physical attributes of computers and memory is that physical attributes are tangible whereas memory attributes are intangible. Both the memory attributes and physical attributes depend on each other. They both work together to accomplish a function. The memory attributes are referred to as central processor and arithmetic logical unit. The processor (CPU) is the central processing unit that perform all the processing of information and part of the CPU is the Arithmetic Logical Unit which perform all calculation: everything that involve calculations. The CPU can be referred to the core of the system. The physical attributes are components such as wire, printers, disc drives, USB, tape drives, telephones, diskettes, discs or any part of the computer that one can touch.

CONCLUSIONS

SUMMARY

The early building of personal computers is the episode of discovery curve. There was an opportunity for growth within the industry. It seems they were no problems that could really under mind the development of personal computers.

Starting a business should be considered by the experience management team as the development of computer evolves. The expertise of management would carry the developments and innovations of computers through profitable years. The problems of direct and indirect competitions are worth taking into considerations when developing computers because of the differentiations of computer units and services from competitors.

The price of computers should be below the average price of other products. Since home lobbyists or households are primary target in the computer industry, it may make sense to focus on having a reduced or low price. The offering of additional business or services such as programming, consulting, training, education and maintenance must be at competitive advantage if profitability are main goals of success. When consumers realize that such perks or services are available, then it will encourage them to remain loyal customers. Users' friendliness, quality of service and affordability would contribute to success.

The sales of computers may fluctuate from season to season. For example, if about 200 products of the units were sold to educational market during a summer season and about 250 units are sold during a winter season (Christmas Holidays). The increase in the sales may be due to the fact that those who engage or participate in activities were interested in purchasing units for themselves after their involvements in computer activities in the summer.

Since computers are everywhere, there is a market for computers because the learning aspects of DO IT yourself are being made aware of. Therefore the market opportunity does exist. In order to penetrate the market, more will have to be spent on advertisement of computers and their peripherals in educational magazines and periodicals. The distribution of computers from direct sales channel to consumers will be a good idea. But it can be the reverse, that is, from retail to consumers.

EPILOGUE

KNOWLEDGE

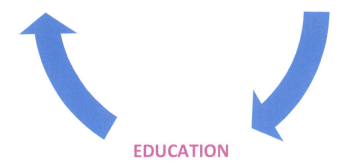

EXPERIENCE

PRACTICE

EDUCATION

SUCCESS IS THROUGH A CONGNIZANCE OF

EDUCATION, EXPERIENCE AND PRACTICE

SUCCESS

KNOWLEDGE

```
**********************************************************************************
**********************************************************************************
**********************************************************************************
**********************************************************************************
**********************************************************************************
**********************************************************************************
**********************************************************************************
**********************************************************************************
**********************************************************************************
**********************************************************************************
**********************************************************************************
**********************************************************************************
**********************************************************************************
**********************************************************************************
**********************************************************************************
**********************************************************************************
**********************************************************************************
**********************************************************************************
&&&&&&&&&&&&&&&&&&&&&&&&&&&&&&&&&&&&&&&&&&&&&&&&&&&&&&&&&&&&&&&&&&&&
&&&&&&&&&&&&&&&&&&&&&&&&&&&&&&&&&&&&&&&&&&&&&&&&&&&&&&&&&&&&&&&&&&&&
&&&&&&&&&&&&&&&&&&&&&&&&&&&&&&&&&&&&&&&&&&&&&&&&&&&&&&&&&&&&&&&&&&&&
&&&&&&&&&&&&&&&&&&&&&&&&&&&&&&&&&&&&&&&&&&&&&&&&&&&&&&&&&&&&&&&&&&&&
&&&&&&&&&&&&&&&&&&&&&&&&&&&&&&&&&&&&&&&&&&&&&&&&&&&&&&&&&&&&&&&&&&&&
&&&&&&&&&&&&&&&&&&&&&&&&&&&&&&&&&&&&&&&&&&&&&&&&&&&&&&&&&&&&&&&&&&&&
&&&&&&&&&&&&&&&&&&&&&&&&&&&&&&&&&&&&&&&&&&&&&&&&&&&&&&&&&&&&&&&&&&&&
&&&&&&&&&&&&&&&&&&&&&&&&&&&&&&&&&&&&&&&&&&&&&&&&&&&&&&&&&&&&&&&&&&&&
&&&&&&&&&&&&&&&&&&&&&&&&&&&&&&&&&&&&&&&&&&&&&&&&&&&&&&&&&&&&&&&&&&&&
&&&&&&&&&&&&&&&&&&&&&&&&&&&&&&&&&&&&&&&&&&&&&&&&&&&&&&&&&&&&&&&&&&&&
&&&&&&&&&&&&&&&&&&&&&&&&&&&&&&&&&&&&&&&&&&&&&&&&&&&&&&&&&&&&&&&&&&&&
&&&&&&&&&&&&&&&&&&&&&&&&&&&&&&&&&&&&&&&&&&&&&&&&&&&&&&&&&&&&&&&&&&&&
&&&&&&&&&&&&&&&&&&&&&&&&&&&&&&&&&&&&&&&&&&&&&&&&&&&&&&&&&&&&&&&&&&&&
&&&&&&&&&&&&&&&&&&&&&&&&&&&&&&&&&&&&&&&&&&&&&&&&&&&&&&&&&&&&&&&&&&&&
```

&&&&&&&&&&&&&&&&&&&&&&&&&&&&&&&&&&&&&&&&&&&&&&&&&&&&&&&&&&&&&&
&&&&&&&&&&&&&&&&&&&&&&&&&&&&&&&&&&&&&&&&&&&&&&&&&&&&&&&&&&&&&&
&&&&&&&&&&&&&&&&&&&&&&&&&&&&&&&&&&&&&&&&&&&&&&&&&&&&&&&&&&&&&&
&&&&&&&&&&&&&&&&&&&&&&&&&&&&&&&&&&&&&&&&&&&&&&&&&&&&&&&&&&&&&&
&&&&&&&&&&&&&&&&&&&&&&&&&&&&&&&&&&&&&&&&&&&&&&&&&&&&&&&&&&&&&&
&&&&&&&&&&&&&&&&&&&&&&&&&&&&&&&&&&&&&&&&&&&&&&&&&&&&&&&&&&&&&&
&&&&&&&&&&&&&&&&&&&&&&&&&&&&&&&&&&&&&&&&&&&&&&&&&&&&&&&&&&&&&&
&&&&&&&&&&&&&&&&&&&&&&&&&&&&&&&&&&&&&&&&&&&&&&&&&&&&&&&&&&&&&&
&&&&&&&&&&&&&&&&&&&&&&&&&&&&&&&&&&&&&&&&&&&&&&&&&&&&&&&&&&&&&&
&&&&&&&&&&&&&&&&&&&&&&&&&&&&&&&&&&&&&&&&&&&&&&&&&&&&&&&&&&&&&&
@@

The Author

Dr. Iwasan D. Kejawa is a native of Nigeria, Africa. He earned a Bachelor of Business Administration degree from Bernard M. Baruch College of the City University of New York, a Master of Science degree from The City College of the City University of New York and a Doctor of Education degree from Nova Southeastern University in Florida U.S.A.

Dr. Kejawa is a Professor of Computer Sciences at Broward College and Miami Dade College. He was previously a Coordinator of Computer Applications at Florida Atlantic University. He has been employed and served in both private and public organizations such as the Chase Bank, AT&T Communications, Motorola Corporation, Nigeria External Telecommunications, Florida State Department of Transportations and Palm Beach County Schools District.

Dr. Kejawa is a professional educator and writer. He is the author of the book Achieving Success in Tumultuous Education; Raw and Pure Education; Education: Leadership in Positive Ways; and Mathematical Intelligence: the art of critical thinking.

@@

&&&&&&&&&&&&&&&&&&&&&&&&&&&&&&&&&&&&&&&&&&&&&&&&&&&&&&&&&&&

&&&&&&&&&&&&&&&&&&&&&&&&&&&&&&&&&&&&&&&&&&&&&&&&&&&&&&&&&&&

www.ingramcontent.com/pod-product-compliance
Lightning Source LLC
Chambersburg PA
CBHW041147050326
40689CB00001B/515